Keepin It Real
(A glimpse into Real Marriage and Parenting)
By
Mo Mydlo

Mydlo, Mo 1973-

Keepin' It Real
A Glimpse Into Real Marriage and Parenting/ Mo Mydlo
ISBN-13:
978-1482000542

ISBN-10:
1482000547

Dedication

I am thrilled to dedicate this book to my husband and children (including my furry baby Tyco my dog). You are always there to add humorous object lessons to all of my books, blogs, and messages. To Tommy, Jake, Travis, Sara, Eli; (my Spiritual kids; Kurt and Angel) and Tyco, you all have my heart. I love you more and more each day.

Introduction

Ok, here it is. This book was dream inspired. I dreamt one night that we were filming a movie at church and the name was "Keepin it Real". I woke up thinking; "wow that would be a cool idea for a sitcom". I can't remember what the sitcom was about, who was in it, or if people even watched it, but I remembered the name.

That seems to be how God talks to me, little one- liners at a time, just enough to keep me coming back for more. So, I just wrote the name down in my journal, then today I realized something, The Mydlo household is sort of a sit com.

We do dumb stuff. We just do. My husband and I were married very young, and we basically grew up together. We found Jesus at different times, and let me tell you, I think God had fun helping us grow through funny object lessons.

I started writing this book today because yesterday my husband and I went car shopping. Needless to say, when you have been together for 20 years, you have made a few large purchases together; you have made a few big decisions together; and you have leaned on each other when you realize you screwed it up together. Also you learned you have to lean on God's grace to pull you out of the deep end.

Yes, this book is my gift to you. A 20 year diary of ignorance and humor to give you the confidence you need to see that God can truly love the imperfect! He can actually choose to work with us too. Wow, sometimes I think; "Really God, there's no one more qualified you can choose"? You have to love God. He seems to enjoy a challenge. Hope you have fun reading!

Merry Christmas, She's Pregnant

Picture this- I am 19 years old having Christmas dinner at my Italian fiancé's grandfather's house. Everyone is laughing, and exchanging gifts and celebrating some amazing family time together. We move into the kitchen to clean up dishes and get ready to put out dessert.

My fiancé Tommy slides up to his mom at the sink and starts to dry dishes. She of course just starts thinking to herself; "Wow, look how well I raised you, you just see the need and you start pitching in to help". Then, Tommy decides to throw it right out there. "Mom, Mo's pregnant. We're getting married in March and the baby is due in August".
Yep, that's Tommy, he loves to share news that may shock you, in front of crowds. I think he learned it as a child, figuring out that if you asked for a friend to spend the night in front of them, it's usually just awkward enough for mom to always say yes.

All I could do, when my future mother-in-law looked at me in shock was hold out my hand and show her the ring that Tommy had given me the night before. I had been trying to keep it a little under-wraps that day, but since the cat is out of the bag, I figured she might as well see his most recent purchase with his first JCPenney card.

Before I could think, I had about 20 different Italians hugging and kissing me, and rubbing my belly. I found myself sitting down for dessert very close to Tommy, directly across the table from his grandfather, who just stared at us. I didn't know what that meant, until I saw that same look on my Dad's face as we shared the news with my parents not long after this.

It was like he was just picturing me 5 years old in my ballet outfit, standing there now promised to a new man who says he will take care of me and the baby, no matter what. I remember my Dad asking Tommy; "So, do you have a plan"? Tommy of course, the salesman that he is said; "Yes, sir, I have a plan." Only minutes later, in confidence he said to me "A plan? He thinks I have a plan? I work at a drug store. I go to college part-time. I haven't even decided on a major yet. My plan last week was to save enough money for the Metallica concert coming in a couple months. Needless to say; he made me a little anxious.

So, yes, we decided to make some plans together. We planned the wedding, we opened a savings together and we started facing this giant head on. As I look back now, I see that it was not God's will that we have sex before marriage; but because He is a loving, gracious God, He brought a lifetime of good out of our indiscretion.

The greatest, is nineteen years old now, graduated high school with honors, and enrolled in college, saved, baptized and Christian dating his girlfriend. He is pursuing purity. Yes, God is gracious.

We are indebted to our two wonderful families that helped us as we became man and wife so early out of the shoot. Our moms taught me how to be a mom and our Dads taught Tommy how to be a dad.

I'm very thankful that they didn't mind that we interrupted their Christmas dinner plans that year. As a mom now, thinking of all of the preparations that go into trying to make the holidays magical for our kids, I think the statement, "I'm pregnant can you please pass the peas?", could really put a damper on that. On the plus side, at least we waited until dessert.

What can you learn from the Mydlos?
Make all uncomfortable announcements in front of guests.

Tommy and I at our first semi-formal date.

Here Comes The Snow

Planning our wedding in three months was not that hard. After all I have OCD. I learned how to blog, do Facebook and twitter all in one day. When I set my mind on something, it is pretty tough for me to turn it off.

We set the date for March 13th. I was serious about not looking pregnant in my wedding pictures, so March was our last possible month before the books said I should start looking a little rounder. I can actually say, being pregnant is the only time in my life that I don't have to buy my bras in the little girl's training bra section.

I found a dress shop just outside our town where the woman there obviously felt sorry for me, and she gave me an incredible deal on my dress and my bridesmaids dresses. I designed a simple strapless dress for myself that she charged me a grand total of $75 for, material and labor. Yes, I was born to haggle.

The dress, the reception, the church, the planning, it all seemed to be falling into place beautifully. Before we knew it, March arrived and we were preparing to be one. I could not have been more excited to marry Tommy and start our family together. We truly loved each other. Thank goodness it is true what the bible says; "love covers a multitude of sins".

We lived in Upstate NY. Having a wedding in March in NY was a bit of a weather risk. When I mention a normal sort of risk, I am talking a potentially cloudy, snowy day, that maybe could slow up traffic a little, maybe just maybe, could cause some guests to arrive a little late.

What happened to us that March 13th day 1993 was nothing short of a state of emergency. Literally, it was what the emergency services call a "state of emergency". Tommy and I were married on what was the worst blizzard the eastern seaboard had seen in sixty years. No joke, sixty years…. It was the Blizzard of 93, or what they called; "The Storm of the Century".

The day before my wedding, my sister woke me and my maid of honor Kimmie up in bed and said; "You have to get up, they are predicting several FEET of snow tomorrow to come, the guests are already cancelling". The phone began ringing early in the morning and didn't' stop all day. With every call, we were faced with the decision whether or not to cancel. How do you cancel a wedding the day before? I remembered making my decision as I was sitting in my parent's room crying when my Dad came in and said; "Honey, you don't get married to have a party." He was right. I was to become Tommy Mydlo's bride, and whether it was just my Dad walking me down the aisle to Tommy by ourselves or 100 guests there to witness; that was going to happen.

I am not exaggerating when I say; There was no snow on the ground the day before my wedding. Then early that morning the snow began to fall, and it never stopped. Syracuse NY, which is where we were from, received over 43 inches of snow…..that day! Now, for those of us that stink in math like me, I checked, 43 inches is 3 and a half feet of snow. I know people that are 3 1/2 feet tall, they live in my house. So, if my youngest would have stood outside that day, he would have been buried in what fell that day.

I am first going to tell you, if you knew me at all you would know, I hate snow. I am definitely a summer not a winter. I don't ski, I hate to feel cold. I would rather mow the lawn and drench myself in sweat than feel cold toes ever again in my life. So, snow on my wedding day, was nothing short of God's undeniably creative sense of humor. Getting to the church by 11am was hard enough. My Dad plowed the driveway countless times, just to get us out of our house. My bridesmaids had spent the night, because we knew we would have to have as few cars on the road as possible to avoid being pulled over. It was literally against the law to drive that day. By the time we finally reached the church, Dad had to plow out the church driveway to pull us around to walk in.

So you know I am a true to the core country girl; but I never thought I would ride to my wedding in a plow truck. My Dad loved it though. Walking down the aisle, I had no idea who was in the pews. The only thing I could keep my eyes on was Tommy. I was just thanking God he made it, and he didn't get so freaked out that he left me alone at the alter. I mean, think about it, men normally get cold feet as it is, but to also have to fight what we did that morning(literal buried in cold feet), I knew he must really love me.

The wedding was beautiful. All of our closest loved ones made it to the ceremony. But, the reception was another story. The reception hall was twenty minutes from the church, so people were strategically planning who to carpool with, to avoid having more cars on the road. ALL of the bridal party crammed into one limo.

Our limo driver smoked one cigarette after another. I am sure I inhaled more second hand smoke on that drive that felt like eternity than I did for the rest of my pregnancy. But, for some reason, I knew he needed something to calm his nerves driving in these dangerous conditions, so I didn't complain.

You could not see two feet ahead of you. It was like a white sheet was laying on the windshield. One of the ushers sat in front with the driver and just tried to help him keep from hitting oncoming traffic, and out of ditches. Then before we knew it, we came to a stop, a leaning stop. Our limo was stuck in a ditch. Tommy and his ushers knew it was up to them to get out and push. They were standing in several feet of snow, trying to push a limo out. All I could think to myself, if my new husband of about 1 hour, is going to get hit by a truck, making me a bride and a widow all in one day.

Keep in mind , I didn't know Jesus at the time. I think now of the prayers that I could have been praying, the angels I could have been calling on God to commission us, the miracles I could have been petitioning. However all I had was swear words and fear (a pretty unhealthy duo). The ushers pushed and pushed and then one of them would pop their head back into the limo with white snow covered hair, and say; "it's not looking good".

Keep in mind, there are no cell phones, we could literally have been buried alive waiting for an emergency vehicle to drive by and see us.
Then, God sent an angel. He came in the form of a plow driver. My husband somehow flagged him down and said; "Can you pull us out? We are on our way to our reception, and we're stuck". The plow driver spit out his tobacco and told my husband "yes on two conditions." Of course Tommy obliged him at whatever he needed. He quickly stated his stipulations. Number one; if the plow damages the limo at all they can't sue him, Number two; he can kiss the bride.

Well, needless to say, my Prince Charming had no problem sharing his new bride with a man that looked like Grizzly Adams, as long as he saved our lives. (I knew at that point, this was going to be an interesting marriage).
Before I knew it, we felt ourselves moving. The girls all cheered and the ushers all joined us back in the limo snow covered and freezing. In no time, the door opened and a long haired, bearded, dip spitting Angel, bent around the limo door and reached in and laid a big kiss right on my lips. Everyone else cheered. It meant we would live to see the reception.

When we finally made it to the reception hall everyone tearfully cheered as they saw us pull in. It felt like we had returned from the war and our loved ones were there to welcome us home. So, we cleaned ourselves up a little, and we headed in to eat.
The owners of the reception hall were wonderful. They tried to help us keep this magical day, magical…..that is until just after dinner. I felt a tap on my shoulder from the owner's wife who said; "Um, Mo, we have to hurry this reception up, and we have to get these people out of here and on their way home. The kitchen roof just collapsed from the snow." So, we turned what would normally have been about a four hour reception into what was an hour and a half.

Since the DJ never showed up, we were relying on the stereo and the three CDs that the reception hall had. I remember thinking *if I hear Carly Simon, Alabama, or James Taylor one more time I am going to slit my wrists.* At one point I went to switch the music, and I opened the glass door to put in a CD, and the glass door fell and shattered…..*could have done without that!* Every eye in the place looked up at me and I could hear their thoughts. They sounded like; "Oh…poor Mo, this wedding really bites".

We hurried through the reception so quickly that I had cake on my face for the father/daughter dance. We cut the cake, tossed the bouquet, shook a few hands, and before we knew it, we were on our way home.

That is except Tommy and me. We weren't heading home. We were heading to our honeymoon. We had plans to leave for Disney World (The happiest place on earth), and for our wedding night Tommy had made reservations at a beautiful hotel in Syracuse. Since, Syracuse was a half hour away, and we would have been literally taking our lives in our hands driving that far, we stayed in the only hotel that was in the town of our reception. We stayed in the honeymoon suite of the Econo Lodge in Polkville NY. No joke!

Once again, Tommy and I hopped in the Limo, followed my Dad's plow truck, and headed off to the Econo Lodge. When we walked up the stairs to the hotel room from the front desk, a room full of truck drivers that were stranded at the hotel because of the storm, ushered us into our room by banging on the walls and cheering out-loud; "go get her buddy!!!" Wow, was I feeling like royalty?

So, yes, we had the honeymoon suite, It was special because it had a sofa. A sofa, really? Why do we need a sofa? Are we entertaining? Once I got over my anxiety of the truckers downstairs, it really was a great night. I'm not going to share any details except the fact that we got a free night at the hotel. Good ole Dad did it again. He plowed out the hotel and Tommy and I enjoyed a free night on The Polkville Econo Lodge! That was the first of many times Tommy and I have joked with each other and said; "Didn't I tell you, we would live like kings?"

We returned home to an extended reception at both of our parent's houses. Everyone from my family's side, including many of my brides maids, were stranded at my mom's house with the food from the reception. Everyone from Tommy's side was stranded at my husband's parents' house with all of the alcohol from the reception. Needless to say; it was not a quiet couple of days.

Once the snow cleared enough for people to head back to their homes, the local news came to interview Tommy and me. We were tagged as *The Blizzard Couple.* Our first claim to fame as a married couple was an interview done right in my mom's living room and broadcast on the local news channel.

I was so excited about the interview. I was prepared to let everyone know the minute by minute details of how we "survived the storm of the century". I spoke the entire time. I answered all of her questions, and Tommy just shook his head and agreed. He said one line the whole interview.

Later that evening we watched the news to see ourselves, and the entire family gathered around the TV. I was so excited. Finally, something exciting and positive was happening concerning this wedding. We popped popcorn and set the VCR.

Everyone quieted in the room and the reporter began to report the story. She shared a lot of information that I had said. Then, they panned the camera to Tommy's one line and showed me shaking my head like I had camera shock.

The living room went silent. It was obvious they cut me out of the entire interview. Tommy and the reporter stole the whole show. My sister Tammy looked at me and said; "MoMo, it's ok to cry." So, that's exactly what I did. I went to my old bedroom, and had a good old fashioned cry baby fest. It was literally the first tear I cried since the first snowflake dropped.

So, yes, God is good. This book and countless messages from stage as a presenter, has allowed me the chance to tell my funny side of *The Blizzard Wedding*.
He loves us with such detail doesn't He?

Now for any of you women that are planning your wedding right now. I'm sorry if I gave you any extra anxiety, thinking the *What ifs* of a possible blizzard on your wedding. You can rest in the fact that Tommy and I believe God was equipping us right from the start with funny stories to use at dinner parties. It really is a good trade for the antifreeze stain on the bottom of my wedding dress.

Needless to say; it didn't take too long after the wedding to encourage my husband to move to warmer climates. We just kept saying to each other as we were driving the U-haul to Florida; "just keep driving south"!

What can you learn from the Mydlos?
Weddings are meant for the summer!

Cutting the Cake!

What's That Smell?

Tommy and I were so excited about our first apartment. It was an actual half of a house. They took an old colonial house and divided it so that the owner could have two rental properties with both of us having two bedrooms, a bath, as well as a beautiful kitchen, living and laundry room. It was perfect for us. We had a room for a nursery for our first baby, and our first bedroom.

The bedrooms upstairs were cold in the winter and hot in the summer; but for us, it felt like Heaven since it was our own. We even had a nice backyard, a sweet front porch, and we were within walking distance of a couple of parks. We were content.
While I was pregnant with Jacob, we began to prepare the nursery, accumulate all of the baby equipment, and we even bought a station wagon. Tommy and I were getting excited.

I began washing all of the baby clothes, and cloth diapers, and bedding with special baby soap so that it would be gentle on his skin, and I absolutely loved the smell of the nursery. That was until the mysterious smell came. As I would walk upstairs to go to the bedrooms, or the bathroom, a smell which was indescribable kept sort of exuding out of the walls. I began sniffing walls, the carpet on the stairs, and all over the bathroom and bedrooms, and I could not figure out what it was causing the odor.

When I would ask Tommy; "Do you smell that?" He would sometimes say yes, but it always seemed to be like when you take your car to the repair shop and it drives perfectly when you get there, or when you take your sick baby to the doctors and they pep up the second you get them on the examining table.
I needed another opinion. So I called in some girls. My sisters came over and I asked them; "What is that smell?" Let me tell you, we had some noses pinned up against the floor so many times, and you Just couldn't pin point it. Tommy tried to pull the; "It's in your pregnant imagination Mo. You are just like a wolf right now. You can smell what the neighbors are making for lunch". I wouldn't believe that it was my imagination. So, you know what we do my friends, if our husbands tell us we are crazy. We call our Dads.

I had my Dad come over to check out what he thought was going on. He told me to have my landlord there at the same time, in case it was structural. I just remember that my landlord said to me; "Do you think Tommy is maybe peeing in the sink?" I remember wondering what kind of tenants she thought we were. We aren't' sink peeing people ok?
Since my Dad couldn't pin point it, and there was an actual smell, he decided it was time to call in his big wig, his plumber Slim. His name actually fit him. He was 6'4 and weighed no more than 140 pounds. Slim had done many a plumbing jobs for our family before, and so I knew I could trust him.

Slim came by the next day. I took him upstairs to try to pin point the smell. But, Slim decided that we were heading in the wrong direction. He said; "Where is the basement?" I thought he was crazy since the smell just seemed to take place when you walked upstairs. But, I humored him and showed him the door from the kitchen to the dark and scary dirt floor basement that I never ventured into.

Slim went down the dark stairs and yelled up; "Yes mam, just as I suspected." Slim told me to come half way down the stairs and when I did; I saw him standing in a foot of dark sludge. Yes, you guessed it; it was our poop. Some old plumbing pipes had burst and our "nasty" was just invading our cellar, and the smell was seeping up through the bathroom pipes.

My friends, if you have ever been in the nesting stage of pregnancy, when you have double disinfected everything before your little angel comes in to this world to grace your family, you can imagine that poop in your cellar, may kick in the OCD a little, right?

Anyways, Slim told me; he could fix it, and he knew a company that could clean it up. But, everything in my soon- to -be mama spirit was grossed out. I knew that everything that was going to touch our precious baby, was going to have to be rewashed and sanitized before that special day. So, knowing the work I had to do, I asked him to get to work right away. And, wow was I glad that we were renters at that time. It really must "stink" to be the landlord when there is a septic back up in one of your rental properties.

Tommy and I went to stay at my parent's house for a few days while the work was being done. Slim handled the mess perfectly and his stock went up even higher with my Dad. When we were able to return to our house, I just started scrubbing.

Within a few days our house was a home again, and Tommy and I were that much closer to becoming a family of three. We actually enjoyed walking upstairs again to our bedroom at night. We were content again. But, I think selfishly, I was most happy to hand the plumbing bill to my landlord so that she could see we definitely weren't sink-peeing people.

What can you learn from the Mydlos?
Once in a while, you have to go down to the scary basement or poop happens.

Jacob in our first apartment, AFTER IT WAS ALL FIXED AND CLEAN!

A New Car!

If I had a little black book of what I thought came first, second, third, etc in a marriage, I knew that getting a safe car came before we brought our first baby home from the hospital. So, I greeted Tommy at the door one day when he came home from work and said; "Come on babe, we need to go car shopping".

We had been sharing my little hatchback that I got for graduation, because the hatchback Civic that Tommy brought to the marriage was sitting in his mom's driveway. It was parked there for months on end, suffering from a sickness that seemed to reoccur many times under the hands of my sweet husband. This sickness is better known as a"blown engine."

Yes, as much as I love that old guy, he can ruin an engine. My Dad was pretty much famous for saying two things to his six children for many years that stuck in our heads; "don't stand on a ball", and "check that oil".

I have learned after 20 years and six smoking engines that I needed to be the one in the relationship to maintain the regular oil changes, and service checks on our vehicles. Once we implemented this system, much strife seemed to be avoided.

Don't think I am picking on him. I know we all have our gifts. Tommy loves to pick on my lack of gifting in the area of houseplants and gardening. I pretty much stink at all gardening. I have wasted so much money and time trying to force myself to become a good gardener, but it turns out, I hate it. I can't grow a thing, and the beautiful Mother's Day plant that my mother in law buys for me every year finds itself at the mercy of my weakness again and again. I thank her so graciously, but I almost feel sorry for the thing when I put it in the car to head home. It's like a toy heading off to Sid's house on Toy Story. It knows in it's little plant heart that it will never look the same.

This year was actually the first year I heard her say to me when she popped over and saw that the plant was missing: "I really need to think of something else to get you for Mother's Day." Praise The Lord! I can let go of the guilt now! You get the point. God gifts all of us in different ways.

Here we are off to pick out a family car. I knew we needed four doors, and it needed to be safe, but I wasn't ready to be a mini-van mom, after all, I was only 20 years old. But, they sold me on a station wagon, go figure. We picked out a blue Escort Wagon at the local used car lot, and I knew we had some money from our wedding to put towards it, but we would need to finance a little bit. Looking back now, after many clunker cars later, I know we should have pushed, pulled, or towed that Civic to the lot to get some sort of money for it on a trade in. But, instead, his mom was so sick of it decorating her driveway that she had it towed to the local dump for parts.

So, here we choose the car we liked, and it was off to the finance area. We sat down together and I was nervous. This was literally the first investment that we were to make as a married couple. I brought pretty much every bit of ID that we had accumulated up until this point; birth certificates, high school diplomas, my graduation certificate from the babysitting course I took in fifth grade, you name it, I had it.

The man asked us to list our assets. Ok, here it comes; economics class; (that's the one I kept dropping in college, out of boredom). I knew assets just meant what we had in our possession as a married couple. We listed our checking account, and the little bit of wedding savings that we had, then we looked at each other and I just remember Tommy saying to him; "We have a bed." Oh, we were proud of that bed. Tommy's grandfather bought us that bed for our wedding gift, and we knew it had to be expensive. Yes, that's it my friends; we had some hand-me down dishes, plates, couches and chairs, a couple crates to use as end tables, a closet full of clothes; and "A Bed".

That was our asset line on our application, and guess what? We got the car. Turns out, they will turn those 1985 Ford Wagons over to anyone with a pulse, and a bed. I think the guy might have felt bad for us. He may have even made up a few more assets just to make it look better. Maybe he added a "dresser".

What can you learn from the Mydlos?
Don't ever have Tommy or I take care of your car or houseplants while you are on vacation.

Didn't have a picture of our blue wagon, so I found;
My boys cleaning our first van; "Old White"

Could Someone Get Me A Milkshake?

Pregnancy did not agree with me. I was not one of those women that glowed when they were pregnant. I was nauseous in the beginning, obsessive in the middle, and huge as a house at the end. If it were not for pregnancy, Tommy and I would probably have had eight or nine children. Children we love, pregnancy, not so much.

It was getting to be the last trimester of my pregnancy for my first son Jacob. He was due in August, so I was pretty large during the summer months in NY. Summer in NY can be an iffy thing, you either need a sweatshirt because it is unseasonably cold, or you bake in 100 degrees with no air conditioning in most houses. I don't understand why it could never be a comfortable 75 degrees. Was that too much to ask?

I was also allergic to pretty much everything that blooms in the spring and summer in NY. Normally, when I was not pregnant, I would take some allergy medicine, and feel kind of ok, however while I was pregnant, I was not able to take anything. Not fun!

The one positive thing I had going for me was that both my parents and Tommy's parents had pools. I would lay on a raft in my mom's pool one day, then float like a whale at my in -laws the next. I also had two best friends who worked at Ice Cream stands. That was like the perfect marriage between gluttony and laziness.

I would show up and stand in line at the ice cream shop fanning myself, blowing my nose, with my big fat feet swelling by the second, my long hair tied back in a tight bun, and when it was my turn up at the counter, both Kimmie or Shaunessy would have my large, chocolate, milkshake waiting for me with smiles on their faces.

I was large. I literally gained 58 pounds that pregnancy. Tommy looks at pictures now and says; "Wow, you look like you ate someone". I didn't care though. I figured, while I was pregnant or nursing it was like a license to eat. I decided I would worry about getting back to my normal weight after the pregnancy. I had enough to think about with trying to get ready to be a mom. Dieting-That could wait.

I'm going to share with you a not so pretty picture, because life isn't always pretty. But, it sure is funny when you look back. Remember earlier when I described our first apartment, that it was hot in the summer and cold in the winter upstairs in our bedroom? Well, that was an understatement when you were pregnant in August in Upstate NY.

I remember Tommy staring at me and it was the first time in our marriage, I could sense him wondering; "What have I gotten myself into?" Oh, I do stress the **first** time, since there are many more; stay tuned. Anyways, I had just gotten home from errands or something and I was sweaty and congested, so I went and took a shower. The water felt so good that I stayed in for a long time, but I realized I better get out and get dressed, because Tommy was due home.

I waddled wet into the bedroom and started to get dressed. I realized that none of my underwear fit anymore. They pushed too hard on my belly, and I didn't know what to do. I couldn't even think of going without underwear. I began to get anxious. Then before I knew it, I had an idea. I glanced over to Tommy's dresser, swallowed my pride, and grabbed out a pair of his tightey- whiteys. I pulled those beasts on so quickly so that I could not be able to see them when I looked down. I hadn't seen my toes from that angle since the second trimester. I surely wouldn't be able to see my undies.

I humbled myself and pulled them up. It seems that, the very act of taking a shower and putting on a tank top and pulling on underwear, left me just tired enough to lay down on the bed again with the fan blowing on me, and a cold compress on my sinuses.

Within minutes I realized Tommy was home. I heard him walking in from work. I yelled to him that I was upstairs, and with every step I heard him come, I let go of more and more of my vanity. I knew this was only the beginning. He was soon to find out that I prefer wearing A tee-shirt to bed instead of a negligee, I don't digest broccoli really easily, and I think I actually have one of those hemorrhoid things!!!!Ugh!!!

Yep, here he comes. I remember thinking; "oh, he is going to turn around and run". Then before I knew it, he peaked that sweet face in the door, looked at me with those big brown eyes; took a deep breath and let out a big giggle then laid down next to me and kissed my belly. I knew that day he loved me, not just for my looks. Because believe me, in that stage of the game, girlfriend was looking rough!

What can you learn from the Mydlos?
Always keep some granny panties on hand for an emergency.

Sara and I with Eli in my belly

Special Deliveries

Nothing will humble you and at the same time cause you to be in amazing awe of the God of the Universe like childbirth. In the book of Isaiah 42:14 it reads; "For a long time I have kept silent, I have been quiet and held myself back. But now, like a woman in childbirth, I cry out, I gasp, I pant". Amen...You sure do all of those things at one point or another during childbirth.

I believe everyone has a beautiful birth story that is as unique as each snowflake that drops from the sky. That is why on the birthday of each of our children, at their birthday dinner, my husband and I tell them their birth story. You would think they would say; "It's ok, you don't have to tell it again this year". But, they don't. You can see it in their eyes after we pray and eat, that it is one of our traditions that makes them feel very special. It is like their first claim to fame in this world.

If you decide to do this with your family, just be sensitive to details. I mean, let's be honest, you want grandchildren someday right? Don't scare the living daylights out of them. It's not meant to scar them. It's meant to bless them.

With us, having four children, it gave God an opportunity for four very different births. I learned more each birth; I prepared more for each birth; and I was humbled more by each birth.

For my sweet Jacob, my water broke in bed, so I knew I had to go straight to the hospital. Isn't God cool? He knew it was my first, I would have probably second guessed when to go to the hospital, if to call my husband home from work, and if the contractions were real. But, this way left me no room for questions.

It was a really cool thing with Jacob. Throughout the 15 hours of labor, my body acted like it had sort of a natural sedative response to each labor pain. I would have the pain, then fall asleep until the next contraction came. I labored in bed, or in a birthing tub they had at the hospital. I remember the midwife saying; "I'm a little nervous leaving you in the tub, you may fall asleep and drown."

I never received an epidural to have Jacob for the simple reason that I didn't know it existed. Remember, I was only 20 years old. Jake was born a beautiful, healthy, 7 lbs 12 oz. He was breathtaking, and took right to nursing right away.

As a baby, he rarely cried. I knew when he was hungry or didn't feel well because that was the only time he would make a noise. He was born content, and has truly been a very laid -back child ever since.

Then along came Trav. Travis was competitive from the second he was conceived. I knew he would be a basketball star because that is really all that my stomach looked like until the he came out. With Jake, I looked pregnant from the front, side, back, you name it. But, with Travis, I only gained half the weight, and my back hurt every day because of I had no back to hold up that heavy basketball- looking belly I was carrying around all day. Tommy rubbed those kinks out of my back every night. I think his arms were the most happy when I finally went into labor for Trav.

Sweet Trav was determined to enter this world the quickest. My labor for him consisted of four hours, start to finish. It was a true blessing, but the Word says: "To whom much is given, much is required". So, during those four hours, every contraction, instead of putting me to sleep, it made me vomit. And, my darling Tommy was the puke catcher.

By the way, for those of us who have been to the hospital, what is up with the banana split bowl that they give you to vomit in? Really? I couldn't touch a sundae for years, and, you know my ice cream problem. Remember the milkshakes?
Yes, Travis came quickly, and ever since that beautiful angel made his way into this world, he has desired to have a basketball in his hand. His first word was "ball", and at two years old he could tell you what a "webound" was. Thank you Jesus for my two sweet boys.

We never found out with any of our four kids whether we were going to have a boy or a girl. Both Tommy and I absolutely loved the surprise that came with not knowing. We were just so grateful for healthy babies, we figured boy or girl didn't matter. But, God is so...good. He did give me a girl after my two baby boys.

The lesson that I learned right out of the gate with my pregnancy and delivery of Sara was to never say; "I would never do that." Before Sara was born, I used to say; "I would never have a baby so close to Christmas, it robs them of their birthday." So boom, humble pie, baby born on Christmas morning. Yes, Saraceno Noel Mydlo was born on December 25th.

Christmas Eve that year was unlike any we had experienced before. I was five days overdue and getting more uncomfortable by the second. We went to my Jacob's Christmas pageant that morning at church. The church was so packed, and to me, it felt like they had the heat cranked up to 100 degrees in there. We were stuffed into the pews so that everyone could fit; and I just kept fanning myself with a bulletin.

Jacob and my friend Jen's son Isak were right in the center of the choir. They were supposed to be doing sign language to go along with the words to Happy Birthday Jesus. Well, our boys didn't know the signs, so Isak started doing whatever gestures he could think of with his hands. The crowd started laughing, so of course Jake decided to join in.

I am smiling right now thinking of how Isak and Jake were stealing the show. That poor choir teacher had such great intentions; but sometimes five year olds take things into their own hands. Well I began to get a nervous giggle, and I couldn't stop, then came some contractions. I remember saying after the show that if I went into labor right now, I would feel like I already got my Christmas present. I think those words were music to God's ears; because the contractions started and just kept coming. They were not close together, but intense, enough to take my breath away.

We went to Tommy's aunt's house that night for Christmas Eve dinner. I pretty much sat in a comfy chair and talked to whoever decided to come over near the chair. I knew it was close, because one of my favorite foods that at Christmas are his Aunt's homemade fried shrimp, and I couldn't even find room for one.

Tommy and I decided to head home to get the boys to bed and get ready for Santa. We went out to the living room where I just sat on the couch while Tommy got all of the presents out. He looked at me confused, and said; "What's wrong, you love putting out the presents?" I told him, I think I am in labor. He replied; "Oh, no, you are fine, maybe you just overdid it today." He put out Travis' drum set, and Jacob's new Batmobile, and then he said; "Come on, let's just go to bed."

After Tommy fell asleep, the contractions became more intense. I would wake him up periodically, and say; " I think we need to call your mom, I don't feel well". He would say; "No, you wanted to do most of your labor at home so just go back to bed". Then, Tommy would go back to sleep, and I would continue to labor.

When the contractions become so intense I was throwing up, I would lay there, have a contraction, then walk into the bathroom to throw up, then say; "Hon, we really need to go to the hospital" Then, my sweet Tommy would say; "Just a little while longer hon, then we can wake up the boys and do Christmas with them. You don't want to miss that right? "

Tommy would go back to bed, and I would continue in labor…..Finally, I got out of bed, stood over him with a look that you all know you have given your husband before. This look meant business. I said to him; "I am calling your mom. If you don't get up, I am going to the hospital by myself".

Guess what? Tommy got up. Before I knew it, his mom was at my bedside. She came in so excited, and wondered why I couldn't get up enough energy to stand up.
I was having back to back contractions. She said; "Honey, it's snowing outside, you have to put some shoes on." I told her, " I can't put my shoes on." At that point, I saw her give Tommy the same look I gave him when I was standing over him at the bed. She said; "Tommy, she is ready to have this baby."

So, Tommy helped me to the car, and that boy drove as quickly as he could to the hospital. By the time we got there he parked the car near the emergency room. I had a contraction as he stopped the car, then we stood up to walk in and I said; "wait, I'm having a contraction". I will never forget what Tommy said; "No, you aren't, you just had one"......With a voice like "The Exorcist" I said; "I'm having another".

When we got inside, my prayers were answered. My good friend's mom who works in labor and delivery was on duty. She saw me and ran over to me with a wheelchair. I told her that the contractions weren't stopping, and she got me right into the first delivery room. She checked me and said; "Mo, you are fully dilated, don't push, I have to get the midwife here. I can deliver this baby, but I don't want to"

A wave of adrenaline swept over me; I have to be honest, I thought to myself; "I am awesome!" I did all of this by myself." I remember thinking to myself that, if the laboring is done, I could push this baby out like I did Travis in two pushes, and I could go home and open presents with the boys!!!!!!WRONG!!! I pushed for an hour and a half. Every time I would push, the baby would pop back up. She just wouldn't engage and my midwife was getting concerned. I was so exhausted. One of the nurses said; "What if we try the birthing bar?" They hooked a bar to my bed, I stood up, and within one push, out came my daughter." Gravity baby!!! The midwife quietly and calmly pulled this chord from around my "purple" babies face. The chord had been wrapped around Sara's neck so every time she started to come down the birth canal, it would choke her, so she would pop back up to breath.

I remember looking at Tommy wondering; "why is our baby purple?" She was so purple she was black, and very quiet. Her Apgar score was a 2. After a few minutes, she let out a cry, and started pinking up so perfectly. I just held her and thought; "Oh my goodness, a girl, a beautiful, wonderful 8 lbs 1 oz girl. She was breathtaking.

Praise God, she was ok. They gave her a second Apgar score of a 9, but said; "We have to get this baby under a warmer. She is very cold". You see, the room that they took me to deliver her in was freezing, and they had no time to heat it up for us since we came in so quickly. So, Sara had to be under a warmer for hours.

I got taken to a comfy room to rest, while Sara was under the warmer. Tommy and I couldn't believe how blessed we felt to have a daughter now to grow up with her two amazing brothers. My heart was full. I sent Tommy home to go spend some time with the boys for Christmas morning, and I laid there alone in this hospital bed.

Most people would have rested. But, I was getting anxious. Why were they keeping her so long? This was my new present, my Christmas miracle, my angel. I needed to go see her, so I walked down to the nursery. The walk down to the nursery was fine. It was about four doors down, and I felt ok. By the time I got down to the nurses' station I said to her; "I just want to be near her, so they handed me a rocking chair and I rocked right next to her for a while."

I began to feel dizzy, so I said to the nurse, I think I need to go lie down. She said; "Can I get you the wheelchair?" I said; "No, I am ok." Those are the last words I remembered saying. I made it back to my room, and passed out face first on my bed. The nurse must have heard me fall, so she ran down. Before I knew it, I heard her yelling; "Maureen, stay with me." They were giving me smelling salts, and I would wake up, then I would pass out again, over and over". I was hemorrhaging. Before I knew it, my husband was over my bed.

The nurse had called Tommy back to the hospital. He was looking at me so scared. He said I was as white as a ghost. The pictures were amazing. After Sara was born, I looked like a million bucks, the pictures of when we took her home, I looked like the walking dead.

Blood is a funny thing. We sure need it. When we decide to walk the halls an hour after we delivered a baby, sometimes, we can lose some of it! DUMB! Thank You Lord for your grace!

So, my Christmas miracles kept happening, Jacob stole the show at the pageant. I didn't kill Tommy when he thought I was faking labor. Saraceno Noel Mydlo was coming home to grace our family, and I learned, when they offer you a wheelchair, **take it**!

Fast forward five years. My gorgeous babies are all school age. Within this amount of time, our family had relocated to sunny Florida, met some amazing friends and joined an awesome church, where I started the first MOPS (Mothers of Preschoolers) group in town. Tommy was working at the happiest place on earth (Disney World) as a machinist, and we were content. Well, almost content, Tommy and I both wanted another baby.

We decided to start trying for our fourth. By this time, we had delivered three babies, epidural free, with midwives, and we thought number four would follow suit.

I found a wonderful midwife who had a birthing center in town. She told me I was a prime candidate for a home birth. I was so excited to deliver naturally, at home, no hospitals, and it would be a water birth. I remembered how relaxed I felt with Jacob laboring in the labor tub they had at the hospital. It made perfect sense to me.

All of the original sonograms looked perfect. It was to be a healthy baby, and we would let God show us the perfect sex, weight, everything. We were so excited for the whole experience. Each monthly appointment left me more excited for the home birth. Jennie (my midwife) was so calming, loving and reassuring that everything was going to be great. We were all getting prepared for baby number four to grace our family.

I was in my third trimester, and the door- bell rang. I was excited. It was my birth kit. It was filled with everything that you needed to host a healthy home birth. I couldn't wait to show Tommy after dinner. I began to make dinner, and all of a sudden I felt a gush. I thought. That is weird. Is my water breaking? I still had nine weeks to go.

I went to the bathroom, and it was blood. I began to panic. I called Tommy and said; "I am bleeding". He said call Jennie, I will be right home. Jennie told us to come in. She said; "Honey, don't worry, it could be nothing"

When I got to the birth center she saw how much blood it was and she said; "I'm going to send you to Arnold Palmer hospital for a sonogram". She wouldn't do an internal, and I could tell that something wasn't right. She assured me, these doctors were the best, and that everything was going to be ok.

This was not in the plan! I had just gotten the birth kit that day. What is going on? What was God trying to show me? We sat in the waiting room with countless pregnant women, and I thought; "what is taking them so long?" Finally they took us in. They did a sonogram and recognized that I had Placenta Previa. It is a condition in which the placenta is below the womb, and it causes bleeding, and can prevent the baby from passing through the canal. In days past, this was one of those conditions in which women died in childbirth. Women that delivered at home that is!

Well, to make a long story short, the home birth was called off, and replaced with three weeks of bed rest, two visits to the high risk clinic, a planned C-section, and paperwork signed to do a tubal ligation during the procedure. Hmm, I guess God was showing me who was in control.

Bed rest was interesting. Turns out I am not a good couch potato. I watched a couple seasons of "Little House On The Prairie", "Reba", and "A Baby Story", I took naps, and did some scrapbooking.. Time just seemed to crawl.

Ok, confession time, I even conned my sister into driving me around to a couple garage sales. We would pull up to the sale, and I would point out stuff from the car, and she would hold it up for me to see. I know, that doesn't count for bed-rest, but I had cabin fever ok?

So soon, it was the day for my planned C-section. Bed rest was over and we made it through the three weeks without bleeding and now it was time to meet our new angel. Tommy and I had to be at the hospital at 6am. We woke up energized and got the older kids all set with Grandma. Before we knew it, we were in the surgery prep area, and it was time for the epidural to numb me for surgery. That was about the only time I got a little nervous, but once that baby kicked in, the nerves went away.

Let me tell you, Tommy totally redeemed himself on this delivery. He took the entire week off of work after our baby was due, and he never left my side one second. He was the epitomy of support and love.

The C-section went perfectly, and before I knew it, they laid the most beautiful baby boy on my chest. He was crying when he came out, then when he heard me say; "Hi sweet baby"; he stopped immediately. Having already agreed on names before, we decided if it was a girl, it would be Mary Grace, and if it was a boy, it would be Elijah and we would call him Eli. Tommy said to me; "We have an Eli".

The recovery was a lot harder than a normal vaginal delivery, but the hospital made it as comfortable and relaxing as it could be. Tommy and I had some beautiful bonding time with Eli all by ourselves, and then we were able to bring him home to meet his precious family.

Well, those are my babies' birth stories, their first claim to fame, and the memories that will never escape a proud mama's heart. Though they each came into this world a little different, the lessons that I took from each of them were priceless. There is no doubt in my mind that God is an artist. His creative design for human life is awe inspiring.

What can you learn from the Mydlos?

When your water breaks; go to the hospital, after labor, don't go running a marathon in the hallways at the hospital; if they offer you a wheelchair, take it; and for goodness sake; **Take the Epidural**; they aren't gonna name a cookie after you!

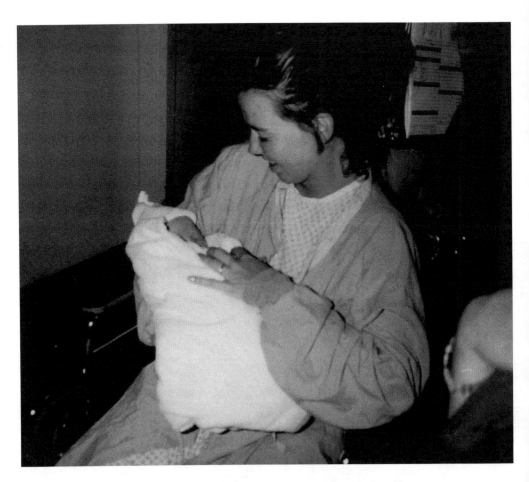

When they wheeled me out with my sweet baby Jake

Birthday Parties!

If anything has aged me in the past 20 years, it has been the anxiety of wondering what my kids will say about their childhood when they are adults. Oh it is my prayer that they say; "I had such a great childhood, it is exactly what I want for my kids." But, I am too much of a realist for that. That whole leaving your mother and father and cleaving to your spouse thing that God instructs us to do can sort of give all of us some fresh revelations on what to do different with our kids.

Well, birthday parties, I hope we nailed that one. We sure tried. I think we tried just a tiny bit too hard with our first son Jake though. If you have to save for a few months prior, or pay credit cards for a few months later, you have gone too far. We didn't care though, it was like Tommy and I had an unspoken agreement that we were to be known as the "best birthday party parents".

Jake's first birthday party was pretty normal for your first child. You invite everyone who has ever known you, ever given you a good gift, ever knocked on your door, ever said hi to you at the grocery store, ever handed you a happy meal in the drive thru. You name them and they are invited. Yes, pretty normal. Until it is present opening time, and you realize your one year old would rather play with the boxes and the wrapping paper than to graciously say thank you to the UPS man for his gift. Whew....I think I was in a full out sweat by the time we were finished opening those gifts and writing down names for thank you notes.

So, by birthday number two, we smartened up and decided to only invite close friends and family. After all, the price of the pony that we rented was so high we had to lower our food budget a little to allow for it. Yes, we had a live pony in our front yard, which was about 500 square feet. The pony did so many circles I am surprised he didn't pass out from dizziness. We just kept popping kids up on that horse's back and cheering. That is every kid except Jake though. Turns out two year olds are sometimes a little nervous and afraid of horses.

Yes, by the time Jake's third birthday had come around, we now were the proud parents of two kids, and well, we realized whatever we do with one child, we are going to have to do with two....hmm... Tommy better get a second job.

Jake's third birthday we invited no other than "Peaches the Clown". She did a great job entertaining the kids with balloon animals, face painting and a little magic show, but Peaches was a tiny bit frightening to me. Most of the kids liked her, but for some reason clowns freak me out. I decided on no clown the next year. I'm still a little freaked out.

So, for Jake's fourth birthday….Batman came. Yes, really, Tommy's friend from work rented a Batman costume, and drove one of his Dad's antique cars that looked like The Batmobile into our backyard to surprise the kids at the party. Oh, and Batman knew right where to come, because that morning, Tommy had spray painted the bat symbol the size of a large truck, in the grass. A little overboard, you say? Well maybe.

I would love to tell you that we soon knocked it off and came to our senses and just played pin the tail on the donkey, but the Mydlo kids experienced a few more eccentric birthdays before we finally pulled the plug on "birthday extravaganza".

We rented bounce houses, water slides, had costume parties (including one that everyone, including the adults had to dress up as superheroes), we did bowling parties, Disney World, a carnival, spa days, and last but definitely not least, my favorite; I organized our very own version of "The Amazing Race" for a couple of my kids for their birthdays.

Whew…I am tired just writing these.

Thank Goodness we smartened up. Birthdays have sort of morphed into Little Ceasers pizza, a homemade cake from their Aunt Annie, and our big family and a few friends joining us at our house for some quality time. My favorite part is we always tell our kids about their birth story each year. They really love it.

We learned that you don't need to remortgage the house in order to pay for a special birthday party. You just need to let the most special people in your life know that you are crazy about them. After all, I was running out of ideas.

What can you learn from the Mydlos? Leave Birthday Party Planning up To Chuckee Cheeses!.

Eli's first birthday

Our Little Sara had a Tinkerbell Birthday

Jacob's Horse Birthday

Trav's Halloween Birthday

Cousins make birthday parties the best!

Trav's birthday that he got his violin from Papa

Kids Puke! Just Sayin!

If you think you are getting out of cleaning up vomit as a new mother, you have another thing coming. For some reason, vomit, and poop seem to be a topic that many moms find themselves talking about on a daily basis.

First of all poop. It just happens to be one of the ways you can tell just what your kids have been eating, how healthy they are, and how much water they have been drinking. First thing I ask my kids when they say they don't feel well is; "Did you poop today?" As a baby, you could keep track, but once those little gems are potty trained, it has to be part of the conversation for a proper Dr. Mom diagnosis. After all, the colon is the gateway to health.

So, yes, poop is a topic that just happens to come up with kids. My girlfriend asked me the other day if we ever played; "poop or chocolate" when my kids were little at our house. I asked; "What is poop or chocolate?" She said; "Well, with potty training preschoolers in the house, sometimes we find a treasure on the floor and it becomes a mystery; "Poop, or chocolate?" I told her to take my advice and always treat it like it is poop and grab the sanitizer. Don't even try to solve the mystery, after all if your bet is wrong, chocolate is cheap and can be replaced.

Potty training is one of those marvelous times in parenting that you better not have a gag reflex that is out of control, because you will be tested. Those Barbie and Batman training pants can be easily saved when you are home with proper gloves and rinsing methods. But, once you are out at the local park and they have an accident. Believe me, those babies become disposable.

I will never forget when my sweet Eli (our youngest) came into my husband and my bedroom one night and stood at the doorway. Eli had just had the stomach bug the day before, and he had started having diarrhea that day. We said; "What's wrong baby?" He looked at us with a very serious face and said plainly; "Here's the thing, I just pooped myself." Tommy and I looked at each other and burst out laughing. Eli is consistently amazing with the one-liners. He can get us laughing at the dumbest things because he has a funny way to present it.

So....yes my friends.....Poop happens and so does puke. So now.... my dissertation on vomit:

With four kids, one thing we have discovered is all kids puke differently. Some have major control, and can make it to the toilet to throw up with no problem. However some of them are like a slow motion Godzilla movie where they turn their head in every direction taking out everything along the way to the bathroom that is one door away!

These kids are the ones that wait until they are just getting ready to throw up, and they start coming to look for you. After all, when you feel like that, you need mommy, but most of the time they are heading in the exact wrong direction of the bathroom. You can't get the words out quick enough; "TUUUURRRNNNNN

ARRRROOOUNND. GOOOOO TOOOO THEEEEE BAAAATHROOOOM". Too late.

To protect my sweet little cherub's pride, I will not tell you which ones are professional pukers and which ones, well, could take a few lessons from their sibs. As a parent, you just figure out their patterns and you plan accordingly.

For the pros, you don't even have to put a towel by the bed, or a bucket near them, they are able to puke, flush, sanitize, wipe, hydrate, and make it back to the bedroom and be back asleep before you even get a chance to help. But, for our Godzillas....you need to invest in tarps, a rug shampooer, and lots and lots of Lysol and Bleach just to stay ahead of the stomach bug.

All kidding aside, there is nothing worse than when your babies don't feel good. It is a helpless mommy feeling that only goes away once their little eyes perk up again and they are back running around the house.

I just wanted to give you a few tips for you if you are a new mom to the "ugly annual stomach flu" who decides to stay for a visit with your family. Number one; do not think you can figure it out! They say the incubation period is like a couple days before they are sick, to a couple days after. But, whenever I thought that was true, and that we were out of the wilderness, a different strand seemed to throw all of my theories out the window. Your best bet, is to just hunker down, make sure you are stocked up in Gatorade and laundry detergent, and don't invite guests over until you are sure you are free of the bug. Because we moms have all felt so bad when we took our kid to a birthday party, and they puked on the birthday boy, and each family there unfortunately takes home a present that they didn't come with (if you know what I mean)......

Number two; Pride comes before the fall people. Don't judge a mom who does bring the sick kid to the party. Sometimes these kids can feel perfectly fine right up until they make their way through your door. Then the stomach bug demon takes charge of the situation. After all, you will be that mom at one point. It's just a matter of probability. Let's stick together as moms and encourage each other instead of judging. Judging only gives God a chance to show his good sense of humor with your payback.

Number three: When your child is sick use that time to get a little ahead on the housework and laundry, because here's the thing; if you catch it; once mama goes down, the housework comes to a screaming halt. I have laid on the couch sick and I think I actually heard my house crying as the cheerios were flying all over; toys were everywhere; and the same kids that gave me the bug the day before, where jumping over my head from the couch onto every pillow and piece of bedding that we had in the house, piled into the middle of the living room. Oh, they named the game; "Pond Pond".

One good thing about sickness is when you feel better life just seems that much more beautiful. Saltine Crackers taste like Thanksgiving dinner; a shower feels like Heaven on Earth, and your loved ones appear more precious to you than they ever did before.

Then a year later…..you puke again! Kids Puke! Just sayin!

What you can learn from the Mydlos? When you play poop or chocolate, always bet on poop.

School Days!

Nothing will make a grown woman cry like her baby's first day of school. I remember each and every one of my children's first days. They all were joyful, excited and ready; mama, not so much.

We have a video of my Jacob's first day, and I still make myself nervous watching myself on that video. You can see me labeling with permanent marker, everything that was not glued down. There's something about organization and labeling that can make a nervous mommy calm down a little bit. CONTROL FREAK!

On the video I reminded Jake about 10 times that he is to never talk or ride with a stranger. You can just see him with this glazed over look like; "Dad, can you make her stop?" He was just excited about the goodies I had stuck in his lunchbox for snacks. Hd had not a worry in the world.

I would like to tell you that it gets easier the more children you have, but you still have the same worries that you do with your first. I have just learned how to overcome them with prayer and with the Word of God. I still pray over each and every one of my kids every day and I will continue to until I am home with the Lord. That is one thing that will not change!

What has changed though is the time I have to volunteer in the classroom. Tommy and I realized that we literally have one child in each school this year; a college student, a high school student, a middle school student and an elementary school student.

I have to get all of my volunteer hours in at my kids' school by helping chaperone occasional field trips and by helping at the end of the year carnival each year. Speaking of the carnival, that reminds me of a funny story. You knew I was going somewhere with this right?

A couple years ago I was signed up for what I considered the smartest volunteer opportunity at the carnival, I worked in the "prize palace" in the air conditioned library. At Prize Palace the students would come in and redeem their prizes from what they won at all of the different carnival games. I simply had to hang out in there with Eli (who was a baby at the time), and collect tickets, and hand out toys! Easy as pie! Or so I thought!

I arrived at my station early so that I could meet my mom there who would walk my other kids around the carnival to enjoy the event. I had the stroller parked in the library with my purse and Eli's diapers and such in the back. The kids and I were just visiting with a few people who started showing up a little at a time.

A woman came in with her son and she was going through the librarian's desk, so I figured she was the librarian. She soon made her way out of the room, and I never thought another thing about it. My kids asked if we could go purchase their wristbands so I grabbed my purse and we all walked up to the front of the school to get them all set with their wristbands.

When we returned to the library, Jake stayed to help me, as the carnival games were a little young for him. I placed my purse in the back of the stroller, and started working. I was enjoying just talking with the kids and the parents as they came in. My mom and the kids were in and out randomly throughout the night. We were all having fun.

Not too long into the event that same woman who I thought was the librarian came into Prize Palace with her son. She had dark sunglasses on inside the library and she seemed very nervous with her son as she said; "Ok, common, hurry up and pick your prize, let's go".

My sister Kimmie, who also has kids at the school, was visiting with Jake and I at the time that this woman came in. I remember Kimmie whispering to me: "What's up with sunglass girl?" I of course joined right in by saying; "yes, she takes me back to the year 1985."

Before too long, my son Travis came in to ask me for a couple dollars to buy something. I went over to my purse in the back of the stroller, and it was not there. I began looking all over the library, thinking maybe I just set it somewhere else. I asked Kimmie to watch Prize Palace for a little while, and I retraced my steps to the front of the school thinking maybe I left it there when I purchased the wristbands. No luck.

I began to get a little nervous, and I called my husband Tommy to tell him that I thought my purse was stolen. Of course my husband, who has the perfect name; Thomas (Remember Thomas from the bible, Doubting Thomas, who wouldn't believe that Jesus had resurrected until he could see the nail marks in his hand) Tommy thought I had either left my purse in the car or misplaced it myself.

I kept telling him, I didn't lose it. It had been stolen. I told him I would call him back in a little while. I had to look around. So, I began retracing my steps over and over, and I realized I better report it as stolen.

I went up to the DJ to ask them if they would announce that there is a black purse missing, and I found a couple police officers that were there to talk to the kids about staying off of drugs, and they pretty much said; "keep looking".

By this time my friend Darlene from church had seen me asking everyone I knew if they had seen a black purse lying around. She decided to try to help me look. I had to confess what I was thinking to her, as I felt so….guilty, I just needed to get it out, so I could be done with it.

I told her that The sunglass woman in the library was all that I kept thinking about. I told Darlene that I felt so guilty even thinking someone had stolen something just because she was a little odd.

I described the woman to her. I told her she had auburn hair, she was a little heavy set, and she had sunglasses on. So we decided to sort of quietly look around for the woman and look to see if we saw a black purse anywhere near her. After walking in every area of the carnival, we found the woman sitting at the cafeteria table with her son, eating hot dogs for dinner, no black purse near her.

Oh, now I really felt bad. I had just cooked up in my head a thief because she was wearing sunglasses in a dark library. Darlene and I decided to stop looking, and I asked her to forgive my skepticism.

I called Tommy and told him it was missing, and he decided he would call the credit card company to report that our debit card was lost so they would cancel any use of it, if someone did have it.

I found my mom who was walking around with my kids at the carnival and I said; "Mom, I want to go home. I am about to cry and I am frustrated." Kimmie took over Prize Palace, my good friend Kristy kept Travis and Sara with her so they could enjoy the carnival, and mom followed me home.

As I pulled out of the carnival my husband called me on my cell phone. He said; "Mo, I'm sorry. You were right, someone stole your purse." I said; "What?" He explained that when he had them shut off the debit card, the customer service agent decided to go through the last few purchase and times of purchases, so that he could confirm if there were any conspicuous charges on the account.

He told me that she listed; the doctor's office, he said "yes that is our co-pay for our son's check-up today"; then she read the grocery store debit that I spent that morning, he confirmed it, then she began to list charges that were taking place during the carnival at a gas station, then a shoe store....Tommy immediately said to her; "Those aren't my wife's, she has been at my kid's carnival all evening. These are fraudulent." She immediately stopped the use of the card, and Tommy called me. He said; "Mo this person charged at the BP (gas station), then Payless Shoes, I'm going to go to the shoe store to try to catch him." I said; "I'll meet you there!"

I immediately got off the phone and called my mom who was in the car behind me, and Darlene and told them the scenario and said; "Tommy and I are heading to the Payless and we are going to catch the thief." So, of course they hopped in their cars to follow.

All three of our cars pulled into Payless and we went straight to the cashier. Tommy described the amount charged to the card and asked; "Did someone sign Maureen Mydlo for a purchase for $75.00?" The employee called her manager over and they began to go through some receipts. One or two receipts in, they said; "Here it is".

Tommy asked the cashier, what did this person look like? It was only a couple receipts ago, so he figured she could sort of give us some sort of description. She said; "It was a woman." She didn't say hair color, size, anything. She just knew it was a woman who signed my name.

This was the first time Jake said to me; "Mom, do you think it was the weird lady in the library with the glasses?" I have to tell you, it at least made me feel better that I was not the only person who pin pointed this woman as a potential suspect. But, I still wouldn't allow us to believe it without more proof. After all, she was in the cafeteria with her son, and I didn't see the purse, she would have had to have dropped it in the car and come back to the carnival to eat hot dogs. It didn't seem possible. Or if it was possible, she was a really cheap thief. I mean, you have my credit card, get something besides hot dogs for goodness sakes.

I asked the Payless employee; "by any chance, did she have reddish auburn hair, a little overweight, and maybe have sunglasses?" She said; "Yes! That was her".

With chills running up and down my spine we decided to call it more than a hunch. My mom said; "If she was at the BP, then Payless, we have to check Target." Target was right next door.

So Darlene, her husband Steve, Tommy, me and Jake decided to divide and conquer. My mom took Eli in the cart and waited for us at the food court. We walked aisles, with no real plan of what to do if we saw her. We just kept walking and looking.

All everyone had was the description that we had given them. By this time, Tommy had called the police and told them that we had a hunch about a thief and that they should meet us at Target to try to catch her. After a couple minutes, Darlene came walking quickly up to me, and said; "I think I saw her." She began to tell me she that she saw an overweight, auburn haired woman with sunglasses on her head in the women's department with a cart overflowing with stuff!

Jake and I followed Darlene quietly to see if we were right about our hunch. From a distance I saw her. My heart was beating out of my chest as Jake and I both saw our library woman. I found a Target employee quickly and said; "We have to get security. That woman stole my purse. She has charged at the BP, and Payless, and.....well, look at her cart. She is fixin to put me in the poor house."

The employee said; "Be quiet, do not let her see you, I will get security. Try to go to the front. She will have to check out, for them to catch her."

The next few minutes seemed to take a lifetime. I had to make myself very invisible at the front while she finished her shopping spree and headed to a check out. The employee promised me they wouldn't lose her and that they would get her on the security cameras to make sure she didn't leave.

I told my mom to stay at the café with Eli so that they were safe. I went to the customer service counter and began talking to the employee there quietly about what was going on. I faced her so that *Library woman* wouldn't see my face and get scared and walk out.

Before long, the customer service agent said; "Is this her?" I turned around quietly and said; Yes then I turned back toward the agent to be safe. The customer service agent kept giving me a play by play of the things she was trying to buy. I was getting more and more annoyed as things like coffee makers, towels, shoes, clothes, you name it were being checked out with the intention of Tommy and me picking up the bill.

By this time, I would have thought I would have seen police officers, swat cars, something, but all I saw was this woman on a shopping spree, having a ball. Then all of the sudden, they gave her the total, she swiped the card, and it was denied.

She realized the card had been stopped, so she said; "It's ok, I don't need any of it", and she began to walk quickly out the doors past me. I saw no one follow her and I thought she was going to get away! So, I turned around and began to follow her. I don't know what supernatural strength came over me, but I called out to her; "Excuse me mam?" (I mean of course, one still needs to have manners). "Excuse me mam?" She turned around and I said; "Are you Maureen Mydlo?" She said nothing. I continued; "Because I am Maureen Mydlo, and you stole my purse at the carnival, you charged at the BP, and at Payless and", before I knew it there were police officers on every side of me, and her. It was like they came out of nowhere. I finished with; "And these men would like to speak with you." I then took what felt like the first breath I had taken in an hour, and they placed the handcuffs on her. One of the police officers turned to me and said; "Nice take-down."

After a few minutes in the parking lot identifying my belongings in the back of her car, they returned my purse to me with everything in it but my license and debit card that were in her hands when they apprehended her. The police officer looked at the picture and said; "Yes, this looks like you, and he handed it to me".

Tommy, Darlene and Steve, my mom, Jake, Eli and I returned home to my house to celebrate. We could not stop telling the story to everyone about foiling what was not only one crime that night. It turned out that the next day when I spoke to my friend who is the school nurse at our school, she said our librarian had reported that her wallet was stolen from the library along with a few other items. I was able to give them our *library lady's* information and they recouped her belongings as well.

I love telling the story of the night that Darlene and I felt like "Cagney and Lacey". I learned that night that God will sometimes show us things if we will be sensitive to His leading. He is the God that brings all things into the light. He just sometimes needs us to take a few risks to follow His plans for our lives.

When Tommy tells the story, he always adds a fake ending though. He likes to put in there that the lady from the back seat of the police car says; "I would have gotten away with it too, if it wasn't for you pesky kids and your dog."I don't know, I guess it's from Scooby Doo!

What you can learn from the Mydlos? Carry a fanny pack to school carnivals instead of a purse.

Travis at his awards assembly

Eli's Preschool Graduation

Sara's Honor Roll Awards

Jake's High School Graduation

Take Me Out To The Ballgame!

Sports! The Mydlos love them! I would even venture to say that we are slightly competitive. Those who know me would probably say that is an understatement. There isn't a large family gathering at my house without some sort of competitive game as the main event. We love volleyball, flag football, softball, maybe even a hoop shoot contest. Yes, we love sports.

It's not just my boys either. I would have to say Sara and I have probably been called with more technical fouls than anyone else in the family. We blame it on the fact that we have to play a little bit harder with four other boys in the family. I can honestly say only one broken bone has happened in the Mydlo family due to a sporting event, and that was mine.

I broke my finger in a friendly game of kickball with the Pastor and his family. It was a fly ball by the Pastor, and you better believe I was not going to drop that baby! I sacrificed my middle finger in the meantime.....but, he was out!

Yes, you can definitely hear Tommy and I in the stands at our kids games. That is our favorite past-time watching our kids play sports, especially basketball. I can promise you one thing; our kids will never sit in a therapist's chair because mom and dad never attended one of their sporting events. They may sit in the therapist's chair because we attended the events. Who knows? Hope not!

We are very positive though I promise, just loud and positive! Tommy has cracked up a few times at games when women have come up to me while I was engrossed in the game to tap on my shoulder and say; "Wow, I really liked that message you gave at the women's event". It sort of brings me back to reality that we are not at the Olympics competing for the gold. I'm in my kid's gym, at a home game, and I better quiet down a little bit or I may never get invited to preach at another women's event ever again.

Yes, I love watching and playing sports. Sporting events just get those endorphins flowing so naturally. It just makes you feel good. I remember one of my daughter's basketball games and we decided to tape it so she could watch herself later. She was so excited as she pulled the video up when we got home. I was in the kitchen making dinner and all I could hear was my big fat mouth in the back round. You couldn't hear anyone else in the crowd, just me; "Go Sara! That's my girl! Get the ball! Run Baby! Keep Going! Make that shot! Oh, good try Sara! You Go Baby! Yay Baby Girl!" It just kept going! I peeked into the living room and said; "Sorry babe, mama gets excited."

Backyard games are the best. For Fourth of July Tommy gets out the measuring tape and you better believe we have spray painted, regulation lines for our volleyball court. Everyone gets so excited when they pull up and see the net in the side yard. Thanksgiving, we have spray painted football yard lines, and basketball season lasts all year on our cement basketball pad we have laid directly outside the house.

Yes, our family loves sports. We enjoy going to Yankee Games when we visit NY, and Orlando Magic games when can find the time to score some cheap seats. But, most of our sporting events are not professional teams, just the people we love, throwing on some sneakers, and heading outside to bond over some good old fashioned fresh air.

You know I have to tell you a funny sporting story though right? There has to be some sort of embarrassing moment involved or I would have never included it in

"Keepin' it Real". There has to be some little teachable moment so you can learn from the Mydlos what never to do at a sporting event in the future.

So, here it is. My daughter loves her P.E. teacher. Mr. A is wonderful. He loves the kids. He is kind, and funny, and he makes P.E. fun, even for a middle-schooler. Well, Mr. A shared with a couple of his students that he is getting ready to pop the question to his girlfriend. The kids knew her as she had been in to visit a few times at games and during school. So, Sara was so excited for Mr. A. She came home to tell me, and she even told me she was going to give him some tips on how to pop the question.

Sara had told me at one point that his girlfriend lived in another state, and that they had a long distance relationship, but she was moving to Florida. I didn't think anything of it. Well, one afternoon at a volleyball game, I saw Mr. A there. He was talking to a few of Sara's teachers who we are friends with, so I walked over to say hi.

I couldn't help but say to him; "Hey, Mr. A, I heard congratulations will be in order soon". When all of a sudden I saw Sara's eyes get huge, and Mr. A's eyes do the same, as he sort of nodded his head to the left, pointing out the woman standing two people away ....his girlfriend!

It still feels like a blur. I thought she didn't live nearby, and that she was one of the teachers at the school. As for her, her face lit up, like she just won the lottery. After all, a complete stranger just told her that the man she has been waiting to pop the question, is planning to do so soon. Mr. A just turned a little pale.

All Sara said was; "Mom!" That was enough. I knew I blew the surprise. It was one of those times when you ask a woman who has a two year old and isn't pregnant; "When are you due?" It was too late, I couldn't skirt around it. I just had to say; "So sorry! I didn't know you lived nearby." "Mr. A, I am so sorry if I ruined the surprise" They both just started to laugh and he said; "No, she knows it's coming soon." *Well, now she does!*

My friends, I am a Christian author and speaker. So, it makes perfect sense why Satan tries to get me into trouble with the very tool that God is trying to use. I can almost hear God just take a deep sigh in moments like this. As if He just asks Himself; "Whew, this is what I'm working with?"

Yes, I still giggle with Mr. A sometimes when I see him. I tell him. "Hey, if you have any birthday surprises, or surprise parties you want me to tell anyone about, just let me know. I'm here to help."

What you can learn from the Mydlos;

When you show up at the Mydlo's house have your sneakers on ready to play, and be prepared for Mo to say something embarrassing.

Travis Mydlo's first word was ball!

Eli in his first tee-ball league

The Miracles of Vacationing

If there is one thing that both Tommy and I learned from our parents, it was that family vacations are extremely important. Both of our families vacationed differently, but the core belief of making memories that will last a lifetime was shared by both. We try to vacation at least one week each year as a family.

Tommy and I use some of our tax return each year to take our family away for Spring Break. Now that we live in Florida, it is easier on the budget because we don't have to figure in plane tickets. We simply pick a resort at one of our amazing Florida beaches and we live for 7 days like Jimmy Buffet, barefoot and carefree.

This year our family vacation couldn't come quickly enough. I was very burned out from a busy year working outreach and so I splurged a little when I booked our condo. We took the upgrade and had the Penthouse. The pictures were amazing and I could not wait to get there.

We invited my mother in law and my boys' best friend Juan, and we started packing. It was the week before we were getting ready to leave and I got a call from my assistant at work. She said; "Say no if it is too much, but I have a proposition for you". She told me that the church was looking to fly in a Pastor and his family from Colorado who was interviewing for our new Children's Pastor position; but because of it being Spring Break time in Florida, they couldn't find an empty hotel in town.

My assistant Jean said; "I told them that you and your family weren't going to be in your house; so maybe they could pay you what they would have paid for a hotel and you could let them stay at your house." Well, the thought of a little extra money in my paycheck to come home to after vacation was more than I could turn down so I said; "sure." It turned out that they would be coming in right about when we would be leaving, so it was perfect. It was just up to me to get Jean my key, and have her show them where to go.

Ok, how do I start this? Remember I am a little obsessive ok? Well, whenever we leave for vacation one of my favorite things is to leave the house nice and clean to come home to. Who likes to come home from vacation to laundry and stinky dishes you forgot right? But, this time I was not only leaving my house clean to be empty, I was sort of leaving my house to be like a bed and breakfast for guests who I don't know, so my inner clean freak came out.

I started thinking of closets that needed cleaning, then of course the molding needed wiping, the blinds needed dusting, the fan blades were dirty, and then I moved to pantries needing organizing, fridge needed cleaning out, oven needed cleaning, and I even moved to organizing cabinets. Because goodness I would be embarrassed if they thought I didn't know how to organize plates and cups right?

I was obsessed with the pool being ready for their enjoyment and I even laid contact paper in a couple cabinets that weren't to my liking. Whew….I'm tired just talking about my cleaning frenzy. But, here comes the good part.

I was organizing the medicine cabinet, checking expiration dates and throwing away old stuff when I saw something shiny staring at me in the face. It was gold. I reached in and realized it was Tommy's wedding ring. I didn't think anything of it, I figured he was working with something and took off his ring to wash his hands, and just forgot it.

Tommy was working from home so I popped into his office quietly as he was on the phone and I showed him the ring. I whispered; "been looking for this?" He nodded and mouthed thank you to me, and I got back to work.

A couple minutes later, I was folding clothes and putting them in the hall closet when Tommy came up to me and said; "can I talk to you?" I stopped what I was doing and he said; "Mo, where did you find that ring?" I told him the medicine cabinet above the stove in the kitchen.

He said first of all I have to confess something to you. I thought; "*Ok, here we go, confession time*". I thought he was going to just say, he had been looking for it for a while, or some other normal husband thing. But, this was better.

Tommy began; "When we lived in NY (14 years ago) I lost my wedding ring and I was afraid you would be mad so I went and bought another cheap one to replace it, I have had that one ever since." I said; "No biggie, do you feel better?" He said; "I'm not finished. That second ring, I pawned a couple weeks ago so that we would have some extra money to sign Eli up for baseball because I knew how important it was to you that he play."

I kept listening. He said; "this is my original wedding ring from NY!" I looked at him questioning. He kept going as if he had seen a ghost; "Mo, we have lived in four houses since we have been here in Florida, how is it now that we find the ring in the medicine cabinet 14 years later, just sitting in a cabinet?"

Neither one of us could attribute it to anything but a miracle. My friends, I am a neat freak! I clean cabinets often, and we have lived in this house for almost 10 years. Even if I only had cleaned it once a year, I would not have overlooked this ring 10 times. Tommy knew he never packed that ring, as it was lost and he had bought a new one.

We both began praising God for His attention to detail, and His love for us. It was our anniversary the next day, and it was as if God was trying to say to us like a loving father; "hey, block heads, quit pawning and losing these things! They are kind of important!" He has called us block heads before so it was easy to recognize His voice.

So, Tommy wore his original wedding ring to our 19th anniversary dinner the next day, and we left for an amazing family vacation to celebrate God's beautiful four creations, our babies!

What can you learn from the Mydlos?

Sometimes being a neat freak can pay off… in GOLD!

Our Families Favorite Vacation Spot, The Beach!

Financial Wizards

I feel it only fair to warn you as I start out this chapter, that there really is no sort of magic in the way The Mydlos manage money. Quite honestly, to even call it money management would be an overstatement. Praise The Lord that we eventually figured out that if you give God your first fruits of all of your blessings then He will supernaturally take care of your every need. But, until we figured this out, we definitely struggled a little.

Yes, early in our marriage, we made a few less than intelligent money decisions. The first that I can remember involves a door to door photographer named Ernie. Yes, Jacob was a brand new baby, and one day while I was home caring for him a knock at the door came and I answered the knock.

This very convincing salesman talked Tommy and I into buying a photography package for our son Jacob in which he would come to our house twice a year, take pictures of our son, give us as many pictures as our hearts desired, for FIVE YEARS! All for the low price of $250.00 cash and a handwritten contract at my dining room table.

Tommy and I jumped. We are talking pictures until Kindergarten my friends, and in the comfort of our own home. Well, the first batch of pictures were beautiful. We were sure we made the right choice, until it was time to call for his next set of pictures and it took weeks for him to even answer the phone. When he finally agreed to come over, he handed us the film and said; "You can get it developed at Walgreens." We looked at him and asked; "You aren't going to develop it for us?"

Then, we never heard from him again. Turns out he moved to Florida to take care of his elderly mother, and we were left travelling to the Walmart to take pictures of our Jake just like the rest of the world who didn't cough up $250.00 cash.

You would have thought we learned from Ernie, but no. Along with our amazing photography decision I can recall buying a frozen food plan when we didn't even own a freezer. We let the sales woman talk us into renting one of their freezers. Well, we ate all of the good meat the first month then I was stuck coming up with about 50 different recipes for ground beef.

Then there was the key. A key came in the mail. This key was the key that may start a brand new Jeep Cherokee. All we had to do was drive three hours, through a snowstorm, with two toddlers in the back to a cabin in the woods of Paris NY to test if that key fit in the ignition and we were winners. Yep, you guessed it; we gave the typical two minute think this one through that Tommy and I were famous for and we said; "Thought about it, we are in." Turned out we had to tour a time share for a winter hunting cabin. We both don't hunt, and I hate the winter, so it actually was easy to figure out that this one was a no!

We have bought too many warranties, too much insurance, too many pairs of overalls on credit cards that were maxed out anyways. We have bought food on a credit card, rented vehicles on a Sears card, paid household bills with a home equity loan, and bought a Sea Doo at a garage sale.

We literally figured out the hard way, that when it came to finances, we needed to get some wisdom. So, we studied the bible, found out what God says about tithing, and saving, and living without debt, so we ran with it. The cool thing is it didn't take much to convince us. God just had a few preachers preach on it, and we jumped. Can you believe that? Praise God, this one has actually worked.

What can you learn from The Mydlos?

If you buy a frozen food plan, for goodness sake, save some of the chicken for later.

Writing and Gravy

After six years of serving as The Outreach Director at our local church, God began calling me to teach women how to renew their mind in the word of God through writing books and teaching workshops. I thought that I would never change careers once I was ordained into ministry and had the joy of feeding the hungry, clothing and housing the homeless and helping the hurting on a daily basis. But God had another calling for me, and let's be honest God is always going to win in a wrestling match. You might as well wave the white flag.

It was tough to let the other members of the staff know that I was leaving. I had been blessed to allow God to use me for the past six years creating a volunteer base of over 1000 local missionaries and a leadership team that was like family to me. But, I knew it was God's will, so I resigned.

The first couple of weeks home blogging, writing, and being a stay at home mom again was kind of overwhelming. I had all of these projects at the house that I had wanted to do for so long but didn't have time to, while working full time in the ministry and taking care of a home, husband and four children. But, now…I had time.

I couldn't help it, started making lists and I couldn't stop. Stain the pool deck, paint the garage, reorganize closets, change around the bible study room, trim the hedges, mow the yard. I was on a mission, and I was whistling Halleluia the whole time because I was checking stuff off my list like an OCD on crack!

Tommy came home one day, heard the worship music blaring in the garage and saw me knee deep in brown paint, loving life and feeling free. The next day he would come home and he asked; "Did you take the rug up on the back porch?" I said; "yes, do you like the new floor color?"

I was loving my new schedule, I would get up early, have my quiet time with The Lord, get the kids all on the bus and off to school. Then it would be renovation time while I was painting or mowing, or trimming hedges, I would pray to God and He would tell me what to write.

I would write all afternoon. Then with my afternoon cup of coffee in hand, I would welcome the kids off the bus, and be ready to be mom again. I had my first two books done in a month, and ready for publishing. It seemed I was in my sweet spot with God.

Then, I think I started getting a little too sure of my blue collar skills. You see, it was clear that God was calling me home to write, but I never really received the calling to come home and become a machinist or construction worker. So, God decided to remind me of that.

One morning I had heard clearly in my bible study time from God, a sufficient amount of material to write about. I had my blog idea, my next chapter for this book, and some of the homework curriculum for a workshop that I am writing. I sat down very early at my computer to get right to work. Then, my blue collar demon showed up to distract.

My computer is strategically placed so that I have the beautiful office that I always wanted with a window. I am not an indoor girl, so even if the blinds are closed, the sun on my desk makes me feel like I am outside. So, at my desk, I started up my computer and while it was turning on, I looked out the window and noticed my neighbor's yard was pretty tall.

My son Travis takes care of our neighbor's yard, but he recently got a job as the after care provider at our local elementary school, so after High School, then work each day, and getting home about 6pm, he had fallen a little behind with her lawn. I looked down at my computer, looked back at her lawn, looked down at my bare feet, and decided to go put on my sneakers and mow.

I didn't think anything of it. I figured I would just write this afternoon. The schedule had been working so beautifully, and after all, I mow my lawn, why not just help her and Trav out a little? I hopped on the mower, drove it across the road, and started right to work. She peaked out the front door and said; "What are you doing? You don't have to do that." I just waved, smiled, and went on my way......For about two minutes that is.

You see, Travis, had been mowing her lawn for about three years. He knew every inch of this yard, what areas were dangerous for a riding lawn mower, and should just be edged, all the ins and outs. However, I did not. I took the mower up against the outside perimeter of their property, and then I heard a giant THUMP. The mower stalled. I started it right back up, and it stalled again.

My heart began to pound as I looked back at the giant cement stump that was hidden in the tall grass. I had hit that stump head on, and my Sweet John Deer was crying. I jumped off the mower, and ran in to tell my neighbor's husband that I stalled the mower and I wasn't sure if it was what I hit, or if I ran out of gas. I ran after some gas, filled her up, and still nothing.

Oh my goodness, remember on Brady Bunch when the kids were not supposed to be playing ball in the house and they broke mom's favorite vase? That episode came screaming back to my subconscious. I had to get it over with as soon as I could. I had to call Tommy. I told him exactly what happened.

Tommy and I have a rule. We don't let something bother us unless it will matter in a week. Then, we may have a reason to complain, or at least vent a little. Well, this was going to matter in a week. Tommy said "Mo, can I ask you something? Why aren't you writing? I know you have been accomplishing a lot lately; but mowing the lawn is not your gift, and it isn't your job. It's Travis's."

Ouch, he was so right. He was so Michael Brady sitting at his architect desk in his office giving such wise advice to Peter. He should have taken the ball outside and he wouldn't have broken mom's vase, and I should have planted my butt at that computer and the John Deere would still be smiling waiting for Trav in the garage. Instead, it was my neighbors' new lawn ornament until Tommy could get home and push it home.

So...you think I would have learned right? I woke up the next morning, equipped to write, and my girlfriend Jean (who is helping me with some of my editing, and marketing work), called me. She asked if I wanted to come over and help her work on ordering our business cards, and the design of the website, and like a dog with a red ball.....I turned and chased.

I didn't think one second about it being a distraction, because I was actually working on things that pertained to starting the ministry, just not writing. So we spent all afternoon tweaking, and playing on her computer. Then I looked down at my phone and realized I had to hurry home to get Eli (my eight year old) off the bus. I knew I would have to speed, to get there in time…..so I did.

I cut through a short cut that I sometimes take, and I clearly heard in my Spirit; "Mo, it isn't going to save you any time if you get pulled over". So I slowed down for about one minute, and I began to panic again thinking of Eli waiting at the front door thinking he is home alone…and I started speeding again.

I was on my last road home, about five minutes from the arrival of the bus, and flashing lights showed up in my rear view mirror. I pulled over and I asked him as he slowly walked to the car; "Sir, I am so sorry to ask, but can you please follow me to my driveway. I was speeding, because my eight year old will be getting off the bus soon, and I need to be there for him".
He was very sweet and said; "Well that is a valid reason to speed, but yes, I will follow you there." Well, valid reason to speed or not, not even a warning, he still gave me a ticket. I literally think, God was tapping on his shoulder saying; "Yes, she needs one. I warned her and she didn't listen."

So, within two days, I broke the mower, got a speeding ticket, and because I left in such a hurry from Jean's house as we were ordering the business cards, we put the wrong website on there.

The ticket cost $130. Then I signed up and took an online driving course so I wouldn't get any points on my license and my insurance wouldn't go up. That cost $30 and an entire day last week. The business cards (that were wrong) that shipped before we could change them cost $50, and the mower, though it runs is being held together by a bungee cord and some prayers. I tell you, this writing job is lucrative!

Well, that night after the ticket, I decided I better at least feed my husband a nice dinner. So, I made a roast and some mashed potatoes and homemade gravy. Well, the food came out so good. I confessed to everyone at the dinner table about my speeding, and my lack of obedience in just sitting and writing, and we prayed for me to stay focused.

Tommy told me; "Mo, from now on, you write, and you make gravy." I nodded in agreement.

What can you learn from the Mydlos? A good batch of gravy can get you out of a lot of stuff.

All Kidding Aside

Now I would like to share with you some actual advice that I pray will add more blessings to your life than you could ever ask for or imagine.

First of all, Love God with all of your heart, and with all of your soul, and with all of your mind. Then, love your family out of reverence and thankfulness to Him! Jesus is Lord and when you keep Him at the center of your everything, He will make all of your paths straight. He will give you the wisdom you need to raise Godly children.

Second of all, always look at each other with awe and amazement! Recognize each other's gifts and talents and accentuate them.

Realize that it took a Supernatural God to create such amazing people. Never be afraid to be honest with each other. Secrets have no place in families.

Tell each other every day how much you love each other! Tell them in words, in deeds, in hugs, in kisses, in loving kindness towards each other. Never think you have already told them enough. They need to hear it again!

Make up reasons to celebrate life together! Eat family dinner together and talk about your days! Practice being a good listener. Everyone has something they want to say. Give them a chance to say it.

 Teach your kids that their brothers and sisters are God given friends created just for them, to support, to love and to protect. Encourage them to laugh and play together as they become all that God created them to be.

Above all, love each other deeply, from the heart! I pray that you have been blessed reading our story. I have enjoyed sharing! God bless you!

About The Author

Mo Mydlo has been happily married to Tommy Mydlo for twenty years. They reside in Central Florida with their four beautiful children and their dog Tyco. Mo was ordained into ministry and served for six years as the Outreach Director for one of the fastest growing churches in the nation. Mo is serious about her calling to write and teach women how to renew their minds in The Word of God. Mo is available to speak at Women's Events and Retreats. For more information about her schedule, please visit her website at www.unforsakenministries.com

You can also follow Mo:

Unforsaken by Mo Mydlo

momydlo@twitter.com

mo.mydlo@wordpress.com

Other Books By Mo

Notes From A Titus Woman

The A-Z of Caring For Your Home and Family

Available at amazon.com

I Go Before You

A Companion For Your Journey Through Emotional Healing

Available at amazon.com

Overcoming Anxiety Biblically

Available at amazon.com

Coming Soon:

Perfect Love

March 2013